WHY SHOULD I RECYCLE?

700030526381

D1324854

WAYLAND

WHY SHOULD I ?

WHY SHOULD I Save Water?
WHY SHOULD I Save Energy?
WHY SHOULD I Protect?
WHY SHOULD I Recycle?

Published in Great Britain in 2002 by Hodder Wayland
an imprint of Hodder Children's Books
© Copyright 2002 Wayland
Reprinted in 2004 and 2005
Reprinted in 2006 and 2007 by Wayland,
an imprint of Hachette Children's Books

Commissioning editior: Victoria Brooker
Editor: Liz Gogerly
Designer: Jean Wheeler
Digital Colour: Carl Gordon

Produced in association with WWF-UK.
WWF-UK registered charity number 1081247.
A company limited by guarantee number
4016725. Panda device © 1986 WWF ®
WWF registered trademark owner.

All rights reserved. Apart from any use
permitted under UK copyright law, this
publication may only be reproduced, stored
or transmitted, in any form, or by any means
with prior permission in writing of the
publishers or in the case of reprographic
production in accordance with the terms
of licences issued by the Copyright Licensing
Agency.

WORCESTERSHIRE COUNTY COUNCIL	
638	
Bertrams	16.04.07
J363.7282	£5.99
WS	

British Library Cataloguing in Publication Data
Green, Jen, 1955–
Why should I recycle?
1.Recycling (Waste, etc.) - Juvenile literatu
I.Title II.Gordon, Mike, 1948- III.Gogerly, Li
IV.Recycle
363.7'282

ISBN-13: 978 0 7502 3681 2

Printed and bound in China by
WKT Company Ltd

Hachette Children's Books
338 Euston Road, London NW1 3BH

WHY SHOULD I RECYCLE?

Written by Jen Green

Illustrated by Mike Gordon

WAYLAND

In my family, we recycle rubbish. We return things so they can be used again.

We didn't always recycle.
We threw everything away!

On our way to school, we always pass Mr Jones's house. Mr Jones is our teacher.

One day, we saw him putting a special box with cans, bottles and papers by the gate.

'This box is for recycling. All these things are taken away and used again,' said Mr Jones.

9

In class, Mr Jones asked us what we did with our rubbish.

Mr Jones said rubbish contained lots of useful things that can be recycled, or used again.

Mr Jones took the class
to a recycling centre.
It had separate banks
for bottles, tins,
plastic, clothes
and paper.

12

'What do you think happens to all the glass that goes in here?' asked Mr Jones.

'It all gets broken down to make new shiny bottles!

And guess what happens to all the tins that go in here?' asked Mr Jones.

15

'They get melted down to make new metal things such as bikes and scooters.

And what about the paper and plastic that goes in here, and here?' Mr Jones asked.

'The paper all gets shredded and used to make new books and comics.

This plastic can be used to make all kinds of things, including clothes – you might be wearing some!' said Mr Jones.

'Most of the rubbish we put in the bin gets buried in dumps that spoil the countryside. It's good to recycle as much as you can!' said Mr Jones.

'Clothes, books and toys that you don't want can all be taken to the charity shop,' explained Mr Jones.

'The food we buy at supermarkets comes in packages that can all be used again.'

Don't waste waste, Mum!

I told Mum and Dad about our trip to the recycling centre. Now we buy recycled things at the shops.

We also recycle everything at home. Fruit and vegetable peelings get recycled on our new compost heap.

The compost helps my Mum's prize vegetables to grow!

Now we recycle so much rubbish, there's hardly any left for the bin!

Recycling is kind to nature.
It saves money – and it's fun!

Notes for parents and teachers

Why Should I? and the National Curriculum

The *Why Should I?* series satisfies a number of requirements for the *Personal, Social and Health Education* framework at Key Stage 1. There are four titles about the environment in the series: *Why Should I: Save Water? Save Energy? Protect Nature?* and *Recycle?* Within the category of *Citizenship*, these books will help young readers to think about simple environmental issues, and other social and moral dilemmas they may come across in everyday life. Within the category of *Geography*, the books will help children to understand environmental change and how to recognize it in their own surroundings, and also help them to discover how their environment may be improved and sustained. Within the category *Developing confidence and responsibility*, thinking about recycling will also teach children to consider others and to act unselfishly.

Why Should I Recycle? explains about the importance of recycling. It includes a number of tasks children can carry out to begin recycling themselves.

Suggestions for reading the book with children

As you read the book with children, you may find it helpful to stop and discuss issues as they come up in the text. Children might like to reread the story, taking on the role of different characters. Which character reflects their own attitude to recycling most closely? How are their own ideas different from those expressed in the book?

The book explains what happens to the materials that we recycle. Most of the rubbish we put in the dustbin is packaging, made from precious resources: paper and cardboard from trees, plastic from oil, glass and tins from minerals from the ground. All these materials are then processed to make packaging, which uses energy and also creates pollution. Recycling helps us to conserve precious materials and save energy, and so makes for a more sustainable future.

The book also introduces the problem of waste disposal and the damage it causes to the environment. Some of the vast amounts of rubbish we throw away is burned in incinerators that pollute the atmosphere; the rest is buried in landfill sites that may pollute water supplies and land. Much modern waste does not rot, but remains intact for years. Recycling cuts down on waste disposal and thus helps to reduce pollution and save land.

Discussing the subject of recycling may introduce children to a number of unfamiliar words, including energy, environment, incinerator, landfill, packaging, pollution, refuse, rot. Make a list of all the new words and discuss what they mean.

Suggestions for follow-up activities

Discuss facilities for recycling in your local area: are there recycling banks nearby? If a recycling scheme exists locally, do the children's families make use of it? Some people assume that recycling is time-consuming and a bother, but in fact, it takes very little time. Children could find out how rubbish needs to be sorted for local schemes, and whether glass and tins need to be cleaned in preparation.

Encourage children to monitor the amount of waste that gets thrown away at home or at school each week. They could do a survey to find out what things are being thrown away, then begin to sift out materials that can be recycled. The book contains many suggestions for recycling. What other ideas can children come up with? Finally, they might like to monitor the reduction in waste in the dustbin once recycling is underway.

Books to read

I Can Help Recycle Our Rubbish by V. Smith (Watts, 2001)
This book looks at practical ways in which children can protect the environment.
Simple activities show what the problems are, and suggest how they can make a
real difference in preserving the planet's natural resources through recycling.

Recycling by Angela Royston (Hodder Wayland, 2001)
Is everything in your dustbin really rubbish,
or can some of it be used again? This book explains about recycling and the
natural world.

Rubbish and Recycling (Usborne Beginners Series)
by Stephanie Turnbull (Usborne Publishing Ltd, 2005)
An information book that explains what happens to
everything that is thrown away - following rubbish as
it is buried, or recycled.

Rubbish and Recycling (Start-up Geography Series)
by Anna Lee (Evans Brothers, 2003)
This title introduces children to the problems
associated with litter, the benefits of recycling
and ways of improving the environment.

What if? A Book about Recycling
by Mick Manning and Brita Granstrom
(Watts, 2004)
A journey of discovery begins when a boy
drops a bottle containing a message on a
beach. The bottle finds its way to a
recycling centre on the other side of the
ocean. Eventually, the boy receives a
reply to his message.